W9-AVC-686

Inside My Body

What Is My Pulse?

Carol Ballard

Raintree

Chicago, Illinois

www.heinemannraintree.com
Visit our website to find out
more information about
Heinemann-Raintree books.

To order:
☎ Phone 888-454-2279
🖳 Visit www.heinemannraintree.com
   to browse our catalog and order online.

Edited by Kate de Villiers and Vaarunika Dharmapala
Designed by Steve Mead
Illustrations by KJA-artists.com
Picture research by Mica Brancic

Originated by Capstone Global Library Ltd
Printed in the United States of America by Worzalla
Publishing

15 14 13 12 11 10
10 9 8 7 6 5 4 3 2 1

Library of Congress Cataloging-in-Publication Data
Ballard, Carol.
   What is my pulse? : blood and circulation / Carol
Ballard.
      p. cm. — (Inside my body)
   Includes bibliographical references and index.
   ISBN 978-1-4109-4013-1 (hc) — ISBN 978-1-4109-
4024-7 (pb) 1. Blood—Circulation—Juvenile literature.
2. Cardiovascular system—Juvenile literature. 3. Pulse—
Juvenile literature. I. Title. II. Title: Blood and circulation.
   QP103.B357 2011
   612.1'1—dc22   2010024676

Acknowledgments
The author and publisher are grateful to the following
for permission to reproduce copyright material: Alamy
p. **15** (© Norman Owen Tomalin); Corbis p. **5** (© JLP/Jose
L. Pelaez); Getty Images pp. **18** (Stone/Joos Mind), **20**
(National Geographic/Heather Perry), **23** (Imagemore
Co., Ltd), **26** (Digital Vision/Loungepark); iStockphoto.
com pp. **4** (© David Kneafsey), **7** (© salih dastan), **10**
(© Kateryna Potrokhova), **27** (© Elena Elisseeva); Science
Photo Library pp. **13** (Science Source), **14** (Steve
Gschmeissner), **17**, **22**, **24** (Maximilian Stock Ltd);
Shutterstock pp. **16** (Cheryl Casey), **17**, **21**, **23 band aid**
(© Isaac Marzioli), **17**, **21**, **23 gauze** (© Yurok).

Cover photograph of a girl checking her pulse reproduced
with permission of iStock.com (© Nathan Marx).

We would like to thank David Wright for his invaluable
help in the preparation of this book.

Contents

What Is My Pulse? 4

Where Is My Heart? 6

What Is My Heart Made of? 8

How Does My Heart Beat? 10

Where Does My Blood Go? 12

Why Is My Blood Red? 14

What Does My Blood Do? 16

What Is Blood Pressure? 18

Why Does My Pulse Speed Up When I Run? 20

What Is a Heart Attack? 22

Why Do Some People Need Heart Surgery? 24

How Can I Take Care of My Heart? 26

Your Amazing Heart 28

Glossary 30

Find Out More 31

Index 32

Words that appear in the text in bold, **like this**, are explained in the glossary on page 30.

What Is My Pulse?

Put two fingers of one hand gently on the inside of your other wrist, in line with your thumb. Can you feel a beating rhythm? This is your **pulse**.

Your heart beats every minute of every day of your life. Most of the time, your heart beats about 70 times each minute. That is about 100,000 beats every day, and 36 million beats every year!

With each beat, your heart pushes blood through tubes called **blood vessels**. When you feel your pulse, you are feeling this push of blood. So counting the beats in your pulse is the same as counting your heartbeats. The number of beats in one minute is called your **heart rate**.

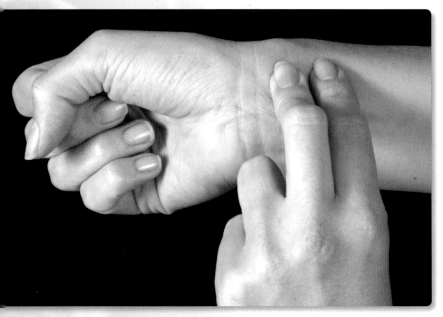

You can feel your pulse on the inside of your wrist.

Listen to your heartbeat

Doctors use an instrument called a stethoscope to listen to a patient's heart. At one end is a metal disc that the doctor holds against the patient's chest. It is connected to earpieces by a bendable tube. The disc picks up the sound of the heartbeat and makes it louder. The sound travels up the tube and into the earpiece, so the doctor can hear the heartbeat clearly and figure out the heart rate.

The doctor is using a stethoscope to hear this girl's heartbeat.

Where Is My Heart?

Your heart sits in the middle of your chest, between your **lungs**. Your left lung is a bit smaller than your right, because the heart is tipped slightly over to the left.

🔍 **This diagram shows the position of the heart and lungs in the chest.**

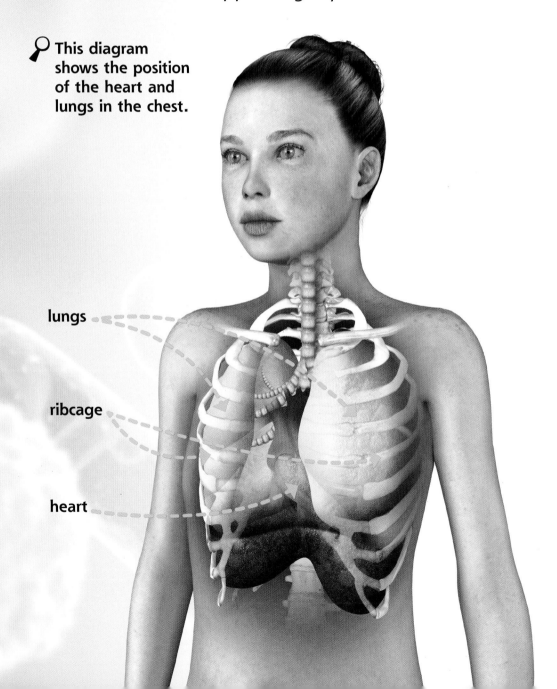

lungs

ribcage

heart

An important organ

Your heart is one of the most important organs in your body. Without it, you would quickly die. It is surrounded and protected by a strong, bony cage called the ribcage. This is made out of your spine at the back, your breastbone at the front, and your ribs on each side. Your heart does not just hang loosely in your chest! Its tough outer layer is attached to strong fibers that anchor the heart to the breastbone and other structures around it.

Compare this X-ray to the diagram on page 6. Can you see where the heart is?

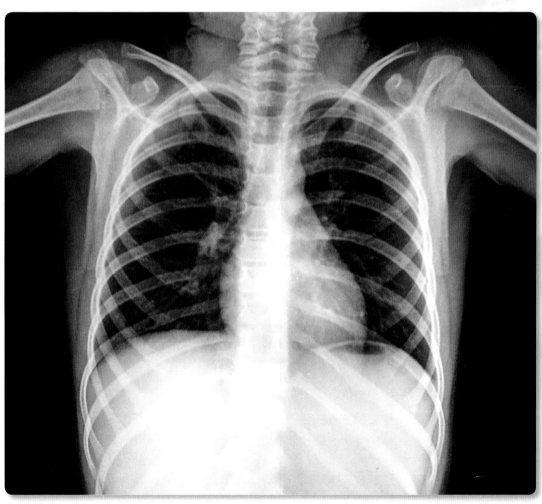

What Is My Heart Made Of?

Make a fist with one hand. That is about the same size as your heart! It is made from very strong **muscle**.

🔍 This diagram shows the heart cut through the middle from top to bottom. It is positioned as if it were inside someone standing in front of you.

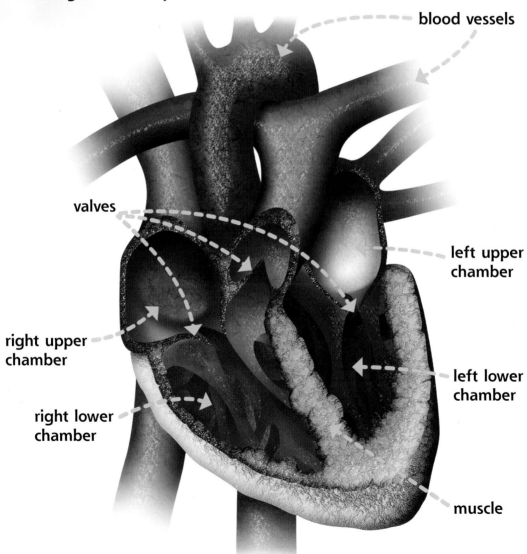

blood vessels

valves

left upper chamber

right upper chamber

left lower chamber

right lower chamber

muscle

The muscle that makes up your heart is called cardiac muscle. It is different from other muscles:

- If you damage an arm or leg muscle, it will heal and repair itself. But if you damage cardiac muscle, it cannot repair itself. The damage is permanent.
- Ordinary muscles only work when your brain sends them a message. Cardiac muscle beats on its own.

Parts of your heart

Your heart is divided into two by a wall of muscle. There are four spaces in your heart called chambers. There are two on each side. Flaps called **valves** control the flow of blood through the chambers.

Large tubes called **blood vessels** carry blood to and from your heart. Blood flows from these through the chambers of the heart. Blood then flows out of the heart into other blood vessels that take it around the body.

SCIENCE BEHIND THE MYTH

MYTH: The heart is in the left side of the chest.

SCIENCE: People often think their heart is on the left side of their body. This is probably because the heartbeat feels stronger on the left than on the right. In fact, the heart is roughly in the center of the chest, and it is tipped slightly to the left.

Like all your other muscles, your heart needs its own supply of blood. A special set of blood vessels carry blood to and from the heart muscle. These are called **coronary** vessels.

How Does My Heart Beat?

Your heart beats in a regular pattern. The "lub-dup" sounds of a heartbeat are made by the **valves** that control the blood flow as they open and close.

This is a printout from a machine used to monitor a patient's heartbeat. It shows the regular pattern of the heartbeat.

SCIENCE BEHIND THE MYTH

MYTH: Your heart can jump into your throat.

SCIENCE: People often say, "My heart was in my throat!" when they have been really scared and felt a thumping in their throat. In fact, your heart is just beating very hard. It is anchored firmly in your chest and cannot jump around!

There are three steps to each heartbeat:

Step 1. The upper chambers fill with blood from around the body.

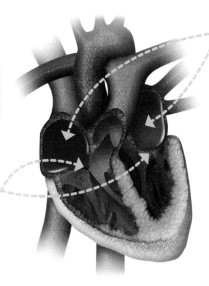

upper chambers fill with blood

lower valves are closed

Step 2. The upper chambers push the blood against the lower valves. The valves are forced open and blood flows into the lower chambers.

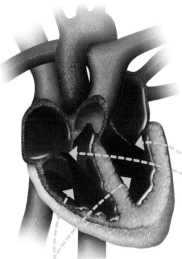

lower valves are open

lower chambers fill with blood

blood vessels carry blood away

Step 3. The lower chambers push the blood against the upper valves and blood flows into the **blood vessels**. From here, it is carried around the body.

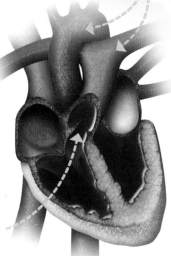

upper valves are open

Where Does My Blood Go?

Your blood does not just slosh around in your body! It travels through your **blood vessels**.

Blood travels around your body in two loops. It flows from your heart, to your **lungs**, and back to your heart. Then it flows around the rest of your body and back to your heart. Then the process starts again.

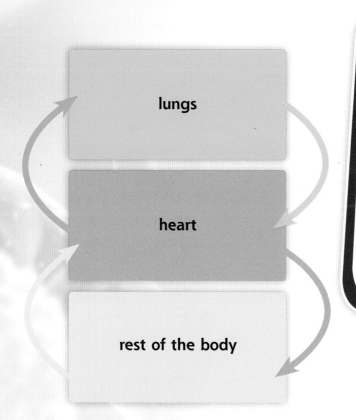

lungs

heart

rest of the body

🔍 This simple diagram shows how blood travels around the body.

Blood vessels

There are three types of blood vessels:

1. **Arteries** carry blood away from your heart. They have strong walls to stand up to the push of blood every time your heart beats.

2. **Veins** carry blood back to your heart. They are not as strong as arteries. They have flaps inside to stop blood from flowing backward.

3. **Capillaries** are the narrowest blood vessels. These carry the blood through your body's organs. They link arteries and veins. Their walls are very thin so that gases and other substances can pass through them.

This X-ray shows the main blood vessels in a human hand.

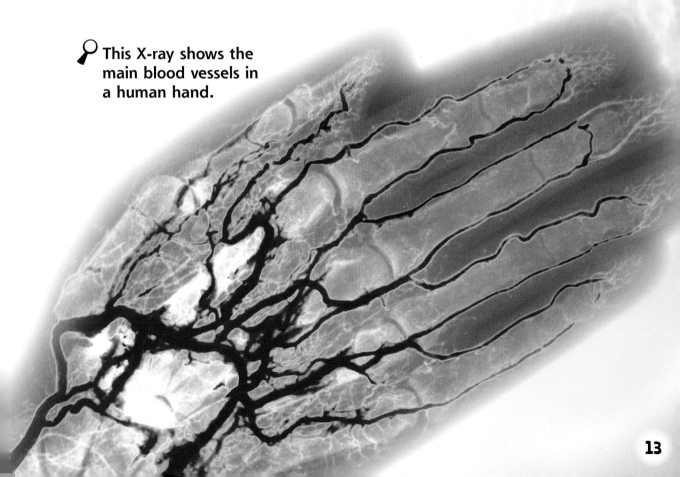

Why Is My Blood Red?

If you look at your blood under a microscope, you see lots of tiny shapes floating around in a clear, pale yellowish liquid. So, why does it look red if you bleed?

This is what your blood would look like through a microscope. The red blobs are red blood cells. The blue shapes are white blood cells. They look blue because a colored dye has been added to make them show up.

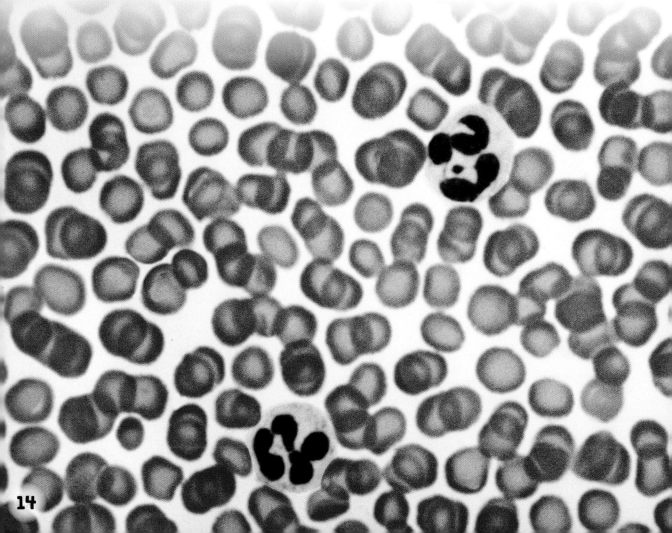

The liquid part of your blood is called **plasma**. It is clear and almost colorless. Floating around in the plasma are tiny blood **cells**. There are two types of blood cell:

- **Red blood cells** are disc-shaped. They carry **oxygen** around your body. There are an amazing 4 to 6 million red blood cells in every cubic millimeter of blood. It is the red blood cells that give your blood its red color.

- **White blood cells** are bigger than red blood cells. They are your body's defense system. Some fire special substances at germs and destroy them. Some surround germs and "eat" them. Some remember germs that you have had before and react quickly to stop them from causing illness or disease.

Scabs

Your blood also contains tiny scraps called **platelets**. If you get cut, the platelets stick together and form a mesh that traps red blood cells. This helps the blood to **clot** and form a scab. The scab prevents any more bleeding and also protects the area while new skin forms underneath.

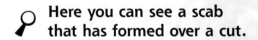
Here you can see a scab that has formed over a cut.

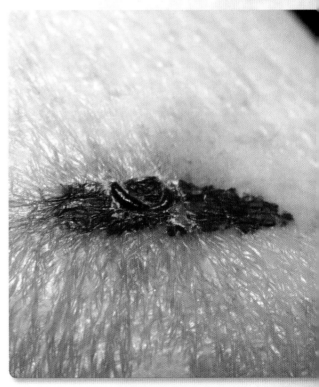

What Does My Blood Do?

Your blood has some very important jobs to do. It helps to control your body temperature, transports substances around your body, and protects your body from diseases.

Control

Your blood helps to control your body temperature. When you are hot, more blood flows through **capillaries** near the surface of your skin. Then the heat passes from your blood, out of your body, and into the air around you.

🔍 **This girl is hot! Her face looks red because the blood is flowing close to the surface of her skin. This helps her body lose heat.**

Transportation

Your blood is your body's transportation system. It delivers energy, **nutrients**, and **oxygen** to where they are needed. Oxygen is carried by **red blood cells**. Nutrients, water, and medicines are all carried in the **plasma**. As blood flows around the body, it collects waste products that your body needs to get rid of.

Protection

Germs, such as bacteria and viruses, can get into your body through a cut in your skin, in your food, or in the air that you breathe. Your blood deals with germs and stops you from getting sick.

Practical advice

Not enough iron?
Blood needs **iron** to carry oxygen around the body. If you do not have enough iron, you may feel tired and look pale. Eat plenty of iron-rich foods such as red meat, green vegetables, eggs, and whole grain bread.

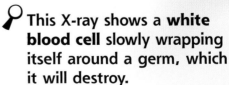

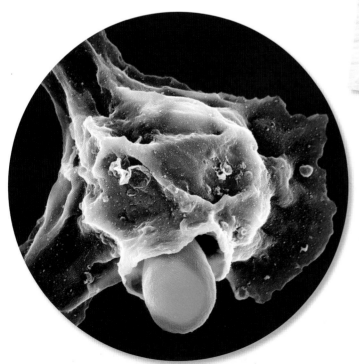

This X-ray shows a **white blood cell** slowly wrapping itself around a germ, which it will destroy.

What Is Blood Pressure?

Blood pressure is a measure of how hard your blood pushes against the walls of the **blood vessels**. When your heart beats, blood is forced out of the heart into your **arteries**. This surge of blood pushes hard against the artery walls.

🔍 **This nurse is measuring a boy's blood pressure.**

How is blood pressure measured?

A doctor or nurse will wrap a cuff tightly around your upper arm and then pump air into the cuff. This inflates it and squeezes your arm. The doctor or nurse will listen to your **pulse** through a stethoscope, while the air is let out of the cuff. He or she will measure the pressure of the first pulse, then measure again when no pulse is heard.

A blood pressure measurement might be written as 120/80. The first measurement (120) shows the blood pressure at its highest, when the heart beats. The second measurement (80) is the blood pressure at its lowest, when the heart is between beats.

What is normal?

A healthy adult's blood pressure measurements are usually about 120/80. Measurements over about 140/90 are called high blood pressure. Measurements below about 90/60 are called low blood pressure.

High blood pressure

High blood pressure can lead to illness. Getting more exercise and avoiding smoking, alcohol, and fatty foods can often help to lower high blood pressure. Some people with high blood pressure may need to take medicine to control it.

Extreme body fact

The highest blood pressure

A giraffe's blood pressure can reach about 300/200. This is higher than any other animal. Giraffes need this high pressure because their necks are so long. Lower blood pressure would mean blood would not get pumped all the way to their heads, and their brains would not work!

Why Does My Pulse Speed Up When I Run?

Your heart beats every minute of every day and night. How fast it beats depends on what you are doing.

Your heart pumps blood around your body. The blood carries **oxygen** and **nutrients** to the places where they are needed. It also collects waste products and carries them away.

🔍 Many activities, such as running, jumping, and swimming, can make your heart beat faster.

When you are asleep or resting, your body is not using much oxygen or energy, or producing much waste. Your blood does not need to travel around quickly, so your heart only needs to pump slowly.

Moving around

When you start to move around, your body does more work. It needs more nutrients and oxygen, and it produces more waste. Your heart has to beat faster to push the blood around more quickly.

When you run really fast, your heart has to speed up even more to pump your blood around even faster. When you stop running, your **heart rate** slows down, and within a few minutes it will be back to normal.

Practical advice

How fit are you?

Find your **pulse** and count the number of beats in one minute. Now do some form of exercise, such as running, jumping, or skipping, for two minutes. When you stop, count your pulse again for one minute. Rest for five minutes and then count your pulse again. You will find that your pulse is faster after exercise and returns to normal after resting. The faster your heart rate returns to normal, the fitter you are!

What Is a Heart Attack?

The heart is a **muscle**. This means it needs food and **oxygen** to work. To get these, it needs a good blood supply. Without enough blood it cannot work properly, and the person may have a heart attack.

A heart attack happens when the **coronary arteries** that supply the heart with blood become blocked. Without fresh blood, the heart muscle quickly becomes damaged.

🔍 **One of the arteries in this heart has become blocked.**

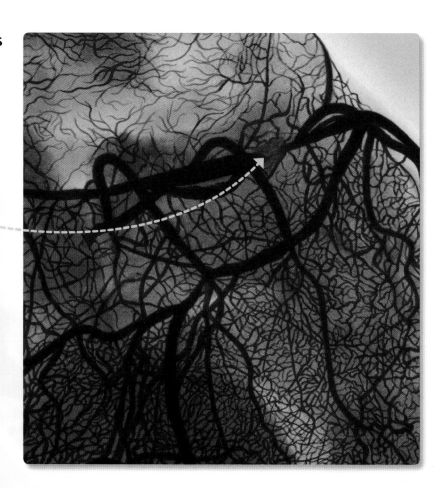

blocked artery

Signs of a heart attack

Many people who have a heart attack make a full recovery, especially if they are treated as soon as possible. Some of the signs of a heart attack are:

- chest pain
- shortness of breath
- nausea
- feeling dizzy or faint
- breaking out in a cold sweat.

Do not worry if you have some of these feelings sometimes. Although they can be signs of a heart attack, they can all occur for much less serious reasons as well.

Practical advice

Is it a heart attack?
If you are with someone who seems unwell and has some or all of these signs, get help and call 911 as quickly as you can. You might just save the person's life!

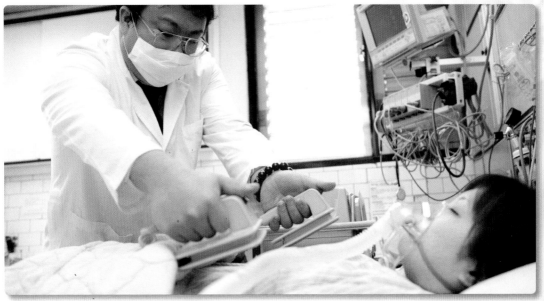

If the heart stops beating during a heart attack, a machine called a defibrillator can restart it. Two pads are held against the chest and an electrical charge is passed through the heart.

Why Do Some People Need Heart Surgery?

Doctors may operate on someone's heart to help it to work properly. They can replace faulty **valves**, or even replace the heart itself. Artificial hearts (made by people) can be used to keep patients alive while they wait for surgery. Scientists are trying to design an artificial heart that could replace a damaged heart forever.

🔍 **Doctors are carrying out surgery on this patient's heart.**

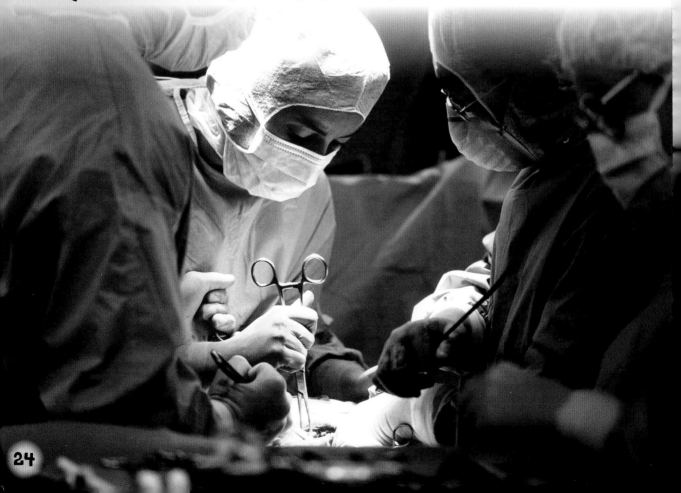

Stopping the heart

It is difficult for doctors to operate on a patient's heart while it is still beating. To get around this problem, doctors use a heart-**lung** machine. This keeps the patient alive, so that surgeons can stop the patient's heart during the operation.

Bypass surgery

If the **blood vessels** that supply a person's heart with blood become blocked, doctors often carry out bypass surgery. This is an operation in which a new blood vessel is attached to bypass the blocked one and carry blood to the heart.

A new heart

In a heart transplant operation, a patient's damaged heart is removed and replaced with a healthy heart from somebody who has recently died. Most people who have a heart transplant are able to live a normal, active life afterward.

Extreme body facts

Transplants
- In 2008 doctors performed 2,163 heart transplants in the United States.
- In 1996, in California, Cheyenne Pyle became the youngest person to receive a heart transplant. She was 90 minutes old.

How Can I Take Care of My Heart?

You have only one heart, and it has to last all your life. It makes sense to take the best care of it that you can. Here are some steps to follow to keep your heart fit and strong.

Exercise

Your heart is a **muscle** and, like your other muscles, it gets stronger the more you use it. Try to do some physical activity every day. Just 30 minutes can make all the difference. The best sort of exercise is anything that makes you feel slightly out of breath.

Exercise is good for your heart!

Diet

What you eat can affect your heart. Plenty of fresh fruits and vegetables, along with whole grain bread and pasta, is good for your health. Foods such as meat, eggs, fish, and nuts can help to build up strong muscles, including your heart. Avoid fried and fatty foods, since these can clog your **blood vessels**. Too much salt can raise your **blood pressure**, so limit the amount of salty snacks you eat.

Weight

If you are overweight, your heart has to work hard to help you carry the extra weight around. Being underweight can weaken your muscles, including your heart. A good, balanced diet and plenty of exercise will keep your body at its ideal weight for your age.

🔍 **Eating foods like these can help to keep your heart strong and healthy.**

Your Amazing Heart

Healthy adults have a **heart rate** of 60 to 80 beats per minute when they are resting. Top athletes have much slower resting heart rates—as low as around 30 beats per minute.

Blue whales can be as long as 30 meters (100 feet) from head to tail. To pump blood around this enormous body, the whale needs a heart the size of a small car!

Shrews have faster heart rates than any other animal. Their hearts beat more than 1,200 times every minute.

A baby's heart beats months before it is born. Doctors use a stethoscope to listen to the baby's heart through its mother's belly. This helps them to check up on the baby's health.

The first heart transplant operation was carried out in 1967 in South Africa. The patient lived for only 18 days after the operation. However, this breakthrough made people realize that heart transplants were possible.

Major blood vessels

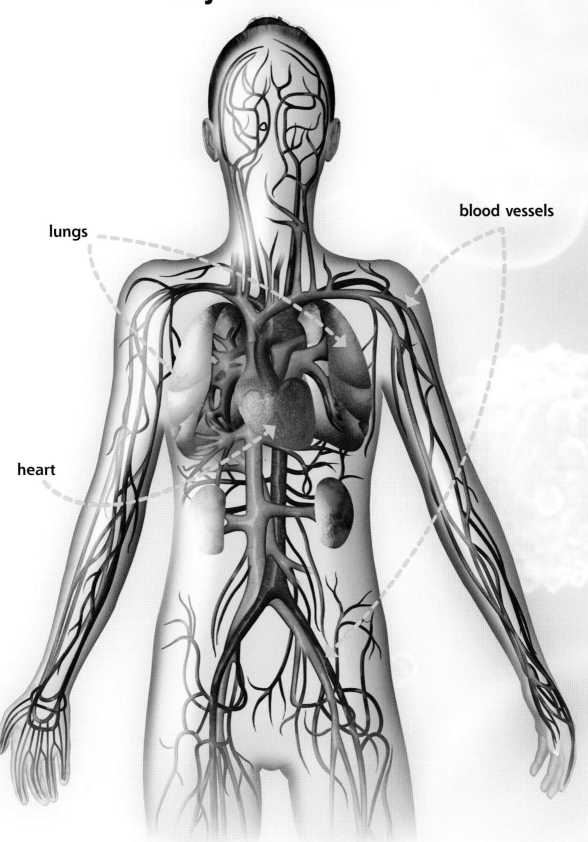

lungs

blood vessels

heart

Glossary

artery type of blood vessel

blood pressure push of blood against artery walls

blood vessel tube in which blood travels around the body

capillary very narrow blood vessel

cell tiny building block from which living things are made

clot become thick, sticky, and eventually dry

coronary to do with the heart

heart rate number of times the heart beats in one minute

iron mineral that helps red blood cells to transport oxygen

lung part of the body used for breathing

muscle part of the body that can be stretched

nutrient substance that your body needs to stay healthy

oxygen gas needed by all living things

plasma liquid part of the blood

platelet part of the blood that helps it to clot

pulse heart beat

red blood cell part of the blood that carries oxygen around the body

valve flap that controls blood flow through the heart

vein type of blood vessel

white blood cell part of the blood that protects you from diseases

Find Out More

Books

Levete, Sarah. *Understanding the Heart, Lungs, and Blood (Understanding the Human Body)*. New York: Rosen, 2010.

Preston, Penny. *Controlling the Blood (How Your Body Works)*. Mankato, Minn.: Amicus, 2011.

Walker, Richard. *The Heart in Action (Body Science)*. Mankato, Minn.: Smart Apple Media, 2005.

Websites

www.heart.org

The website of the American Heart Association has lots of information about how to keep your heart healthy.

http://kidshealth.org/kid/htbw/heart.html

Visit this website to learn more about your heart.

www.mplsheart.org/kids/lets_learn.html

This fun, interactive website has lots of information about the heart and how it works.

Index

arteries 13, 18, 22
artificial hearts 24

blood 4, 9, 11,
    12–19, 20, 21, 22
blood clotting 15
blood pressure
    18–19, 27
blood vessels 4, 8,
    9, 11, 12, 13, 18,
    25, 27, 29
body
    temperature 16

capillaries 13, 16
cardiac muscle 9, 22
cells 14, 15, 17
chambers 8, 9, 11
coronary vessels
    9, 22

diet 17, 27

energy 17, 21
exercise 19, 21,
    26, 27

germs 15, 17

heart 6–11, 12, 13
heart attack 22–23
heart attack
    symptoms 23
heartbeat 4, 5, 9,
    10–11, 20, 28
heart rate 4, 5,
    21, 28
heart surgery 24–25
heart transplants 25
high blood pressure
    19

illness and diseases
    15, 16, 19, 22–25

lungs 6, 12

muscles 8, 9, 22,
    26, 27

nutrients 17, 20, 21

oxygen 15, 17, 20,
    21, 22

plasma 15, 17
platelets 15
pulse 4, 18, 21

red blood cells 14,
    15, 17
ribcage 6, 7

scabs 15
smoking 19

taking care of your
    heart 26–27

valves 8, 9, 10,
    11, 24
veins 13
viruses 17

waste products 17,
    20, 21
weight control 27
white blood cells 14,
    15, 17